Flat Sole Studio
St. Paul, Minnesota

Flat Sole Studio
St. Paul, Minnesota
flatsolestudio.com

Copyright © 2025 Charlotte Agustin

All rights reserved. No part of this publication may be reproduced in whole or in part without written permission of the publisher.

Library of Congress Cataloging-in-Publication Data
Library of Congress Control Number: (to come)
ISBN: 979-8-3484-8609-9 (Ingram pbk)
ISBN: 979-8-313027-59-3 (Amazon pbk)

Credits
Blake Hoena, editorial direction
Flat Sole Studio, cover design and book layout

Image Credits
Charlotte Agustin, all

Blood Drawn
&
Hung Out to Dry

poems by
Charlotte Agustin

Forward

For those who suffer from invisible ailments, falling in love every day, and the bottle. If you lose your mind quite often and find yourself gasping for air frequently, I hope this book brings you comfort in knowing you are not alone.

Tuesday

Tuesday, a quite generic day, there is nothing special about a Tuesday.
Today however, a Tuesday, there are thoughts banging and bashing on my amygdala.
For someone such as myself, today is particularly abysmal. (common)
Funny? No. More like sadistic.
On an average Tuesday you would ask me many questions, probably look at me funny.
It's really not funny at all.
What it is really, is cruel, taffy-like, yes taffy as in the candy.
Stop acting like you haven't had taffy.
You haven't? Well, you're not everyone else in this world so if you could stop interjecting that would be wonderful.
You're making me feel bad. (common)
It's not for me to say his pretty words.
I'd find some words for you, but I'd prefer if the only words you spoke were "yeah" and "turn around" and "I'm sorry".
Then again, I'm quite shallow and wouldn't have anything better to say.

In my head

At first it was a gasp, a chewing of the tongue, ripping of the skin.
Lasting 18 (19 & a half) hours.
I recorded the longest murmur yet.
Laughed some.
As it settled my nails fell off, my teeth became rotted, I lost my eyes.
I slept.
I woke up.
I went back to sleep.
My hands climbed into my throat, my veins fell out and I dreamt of you.
I stopped breathing and started screaming.

Bonnet

Having long hair is painful.
Ponytails get stuck in barbed wire, lacerating yellow skin.
Braids wrap around lungs, it's suffocating.
Fallen hair in the shower pierces through the bottom of my
    feet like embroidery needles (which I had bought for you).
Her short hair sounds sour on the radio, sick, sick, I promise
    you I am retching.
I could not, "choose a better time to meet."
There is, was, will not be.
Red tide algae bloom.
Selfish.
Left me to drown in my own spit and split ends.
For three months
I'd love to not care anymore, laissez faire and all, but hating
    you feels so good.
Better than when we were in bed.

Hereditary

Linda, is it okay to be like you?
When you left there was this song I listened to, in attempts to
    miss you.
I cannot recall if it worked very well, 6 months of TV static
    will do that to a person.
My friend played it the other day, I felt it then.
I was too busy dancing until my cartilage fell out to let it run
    its course.
Do you think she'll hate me like she hated you Linda?
You gave me parts of you, the parts that are scary for a child,
    the burdens as an adult.
I have tried to bury them with you.
They resurface every year like daffodils in the spring,
Although I don't lie as awfully as you did Linda, I throw raw
    eggs at glass doors all the same.
I'd like to blame you, but you can't cry wolf to an empty
    home.
You can't love ashes.
You can't curse the dead.
You can't haunt me Linda, I'll let you rest here.
I'll love you like your parents did and let you rest in my care.

Things are different now

Earlier when we went grocery shopping (different households),
    a girl made me blush.
I thought about her all the way home.
Maybe it's because I'm not used to pretty girls thinking I'm
    pretty or something to the effect of I might just be a
    lesbian.
And then we went home, I was patient with you in a way I
    should've been before.
I mean it is a good thing you cut your hair so no one looks at
    me but the way lace looks on you hurts my eyes.
Lust becomes adoration (unless I'm feeling delusional, lonely
    and stupid).
(common)
It was fine, I didn't feel lonely, stupid OR delusional.
Then, OH GOD, you told me I'm funny.
Which most probably meant nothing at all, just that I'm
    funny.
It's not funny that I like that you think I'm funny.
(it's worrisome)

6/7/2023

I have had many, several thoughts about this mildly terrifying but non-traumatic semi-recent new exploration of a comforting yet an Aladdin's Cave of an exchange.

(words, exhaustion, shared exhaustion, optimism, sweetness, conversations with no proper punctuation).

I have had many, several attempts at being tooth (and nail) pulling-ly honest that there are maybe many, several bubbles of thought involving what is known only as human nature.

Which begs the question, is there anything truly wrong with the sins of greed, lust, envy and the gluttonous want for your time?

Human nature when boiled down to a burnt pot is self preservation and eating.

We can cook the meals we used to because *just maybe* the nostalgia of comfort in the form of consumption will cause your natural human instinct to kick in.

Would it be so bad to love again?

Most likely.

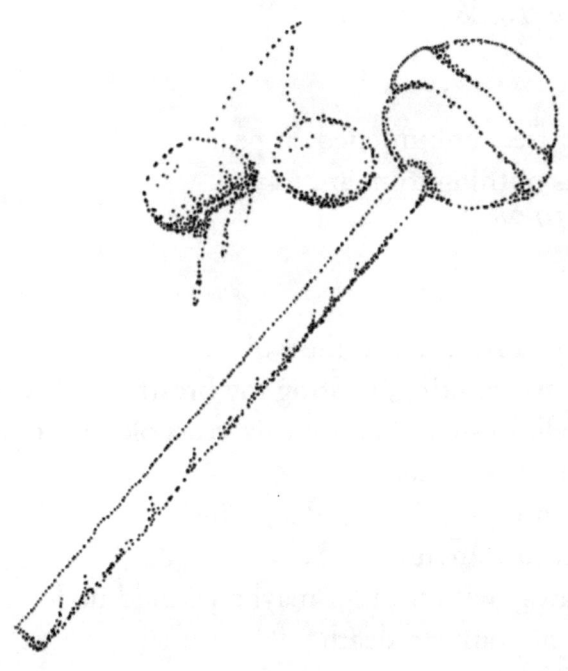

Talking to no one

If I could get away with murder I would have made my peace with God.
    James 4:2

I could be everything you fear.
    Matthew 10:28

They would be free, unburdened, at peace.
My rage means nothing to them, to you.
    Judges 19:24-25

I would've set you free, not to the wolves.
Yet here I am, overreacting, wasting my breath, confused, stupid, small, so small I am but six years old experiencing death for the first time.
I am now left with putrid scars, disgusting.
I am not so delicate anymore.
If I could get away with murder maybe I would no longer feel the weight of your ego death.
    Ezekiel 37:23

Body in the oven

I am the 100 bees stuck in the honey trap the local bakery laid out for me.

I am the heels that twist my ankles on city streets.

I am the paranoia that shot up my nose when I gave into gluttony.

I am the love you smothered into my gums.

I am the weight of your body taking the air from my lungs.

I am the small fire of fear that now grows.

I am the fear that loves the melodies of betrayal and wasted time.

I am afraid that I am not who I say I am and everything you loved is what you feared I wouldn't be.

You are a boy from nowhere that wandered into my world of earth shattering realities and beautiful disenchantments.

I am scared of everything you could possibly mean to me, I'll start early on listening to my demons scream.

If I do this again you have to promise me everything I needed him to be.

6/14/2023

I thought this time I wasn't going to feel this way,
I thought maybe this time it wasn't going to turn into
    everything that has come before you.
The worst feeling in the world.
Tonight I'll have to put all my animals around me.
I'm alone again.
All I have now is soft polyester, a now empty bottle of rum,
    relapsing, and bad air quality (249).
And a chipped tooth.

6/20/2023

Why do we seek out the unpredictable?
Why do we insist on suffocation via one single string of hair?
Why do I seek out what makes me sick, so sick in fact I might just vomit pretty words made of embroidery thread?
Out loud, very loudly, I decided on proclaiming my stupidity (several times).
I hope the neighbors didn't hear me all the way from the 4th floor.
Your hair is much longer than mine.
Your hair looks pretty in the morning (this is because of course you do things no one else sees but me).
My hair is dark, my hair is much thicker than yours (same color as hers).
My hair will probably never go grey.
Her hair will become brittle (mine is prettier, mine is better, love mine more).
I don't know when I'll cut my hair.
I can only hope one day it won't make me sick.

6/21/2023

Is it okay if I lay in your comfort?
Is it immoral to run with the delusion when your hand so naturally lands on my back.
I'm so painfully awake to what you think of me.
I wish we were sleeping in your comfort.
Wouldn't it be nice to sleep in our comfort?
No, no, bad, wrong, upsetting, not our comfort.
Maybe this is all a dream.
Silly, childish and obtuse.
I'd bring you with me, but you dream without me now.
I am problematic at will.
No determination due to fears I choose not to disclose at this time.
Goodnight 12 hours apart.

6/21/2023

Frightening really, how I cannot picture, no, rather, remember what I have done.
I recount very little, what is mine to keep at least.
Lesser so for words that do not leave my mouth.
Those, usually I can recount.
It's not that my life is boring, it's fine (just fine).
Moreso it takes time to come to conclusions, if I do at all.
There is solace, innocence, protection in losing your mind.
Hopefully it works itself out.
I cannot breath well, hopefully it doesn't kill me.

6/23/2024

I'd talk while you couldn't if it meant waking you up every morning.
Wouldn't it be nice?
Kind brown eyes resting on lashes longer than the road to heaven.
Wouldn't it feel right on the way to heaven?
I think we'd fit in fine, once we got to heaven.
We can't hurt in heaven.
Tatay cut my lashes.
Tatay prayed for me.
Prayed for this.
Tatay prayed for someone to take me to heaven.

By Haroon & Charlie—sometime in July

Listen, I couldn't feel it that well.
I probably shouldn't but i'm stupid sometimes.
I tried to tell her I lack love on a dime.
And I come with the heaviest book bag imaginable.
It's got planets, tears and loose teeth, and maybe if you're lucky
    i'll give you a sweet treat.
Unable to read signs, at times appear uninterested but
    completely enamored with the idea of sharing this type 2
    happiness type beat.

A little about me

I am inept at getting an education. Never been a fast learner.
I suck at math.
There was a time where I was always at a higher reading level than most.
Then I started 8th grade.
It all went so downhill, my thoughts became rebellious.
I hated cleaning my room.
I never learned how to do the dishes.
Instead I figured out call and response, less so learning, more so mocking.
I am incredibly bad at listening, a trait I inherited from my mother, something I never learned from my father.
What would he say? I think he would still love me even with my ineptitude to learn.
He wanted me to eat a bagel, but I never learned how to chew.
Again, a flaw passed down from my mother.
She loves me in her own strange ways, I call it "Mother's guilt money".
I can't say I love her back.
Surprise, something I picked up from my mother.
I would like to love her, my bloody sheets would like to love her, my hair that looks nothing like hers would like to love her.
I do not love my mother.
I am scared to lose her, I think it would kill me inside and all the little birds kept in my chest would die too.
Could my life be better if I loved my mother?
I wish god would answer me for once.
Should I learn to love my mother?
Is my inability to learn just an excuse to not love my mother?

7/19/2023

I want to be held.
So gently that you seem afraid I'll break.
I want to be held, not touched.
It burns me like hot honey.
I will rip myself apart if you touch my skin.
Please hold me.
I'm sorry.
Please hold me.
It's not me, it's the honey.
I am suffocating.
I feel.
I don't want to shower and I hate baths.
I'M FUCKING SICK AND I HAVE A FEVER WHY
    WONT YOU HOLD ME
I'm sorry,
I didn't mean it.
It was the hot honey.

7/11/2023

Here is a list of reasons why I'm bitter.
I am prettier but her makeup looks better.
I have better lips but she can sing.
My tattoos are more unique but you touch her skin.
Facial piercings look better on me but he only looks at you.
My art is raw but hers is accomplished.
I love your sister's music more, but she spends time with her.
She is everything to you, I am only in your dreams.
I am lying to myself and you lied to me.

7/26/2023

I often wonder if this heart I have belongs to me.

When I meet someone new or go somewhere new or try something new my heart beats so fast that it must belong to a small bird that is often frightened.

(the hummingbird)

My heart yearns for love, at the same time the mere thought of embrace stirs up my intestines, cutting off the flow of blood to my brain.

I am a hopeless romantic but love makes me so volatile it scares away any prospect of a shared future.

When I love it's so intense even I'm scared, it reaches the core of the earth, it does not stop there, mercilessly strikes through it, leaving it to bleed out until she begs for mercy.

Maybe this heart is mine, maybe it is diseased. Maybe the love my mother gave me is hereditary and bound to pass on through generations.

Maybe that is why every attempt at love ends in a murky pool of putrid tears.

Maybe my heart is my own but not meant for anybody else.

Last time I checked, most birds find mates.

If I have the heart of a bird it is from the body of a black stork, destined for loneliness, an empty nest, and death.

Unfortunately I have come to the conclusion my heart is my own, it seems that the problem is my brain.

It seems that it's a good thing that I am sensitive and feel deeply, that's what a friend told me the other day when I was crying about a wedding I saw online.

My brain is what causes my heart to not feel so good, to become angry at myself for crying so often, so much.

I fear I will run out of water in my body and shrivel away.

Makes you go a little crazy in the head. My therapist told me I'm not crazy, that my brain just tells me I am. I can't tell if that's bullshit or not because my brain is my brain which maybe I have to go to college to understand how that works. I'll find out when I'm 26.

I blame my mother and the death of my father for the lack of rest I get, for my heart being too big to ever feel full, and for being filled with unplaced jealousy.

8/28/2023

This is the first time (first birthday) I have felt the discomfort of growing old.

I thought eighteen was THE age, monumental, life changing. Turns out eighteen is not much different than nineteen is to twenty is to twenty-one is to twenty-two.

Twenty-three however, is much different than eighteen which is very similar to nineteen which is similar to twenty, terrifyingly more similar to twenty-one, twenty-two less so, but still quite similar.

Twenty-three feels like when my lungs were mildly contracted because I was a dumb twenty-one year old.

Twenty-three has become a constant teetering on the edge of will I won't they and I think rather than fall, I want to jump.

That however, is a lie, I have barely wanted to jump off that stack of bricks from a broken home I built myself.

Which is one of the many reasons why twenty-three feels so different from eighteen and so on and so forth.

Subsequently I am so beset by my trembling, slimy, horrendous god awful thoughts I fear falling off the cliff. And I often think I will, not of my own accord but of God's free will.

7/27/2023

The rain feels nice on my cheeks on the drive home.
I laughed when I should've.
I smiled carelessly.
I devoured.
I had an innate urge to consume more.
To smile inappropriately at him.
To laugh when I didn't think anything was funny.
The wind feels nice when my hair's up.
I don't like it much when it's down, it pokes my eyes and
    sticks to my lips.
I'm laughing again, when I shouldn't.
Smiling when I'm not so kind.
Said what would normally never spew from my mouth.
This always happens.
The moon looks at me shamefully again.
But is it so wrong if their words are kinder this way?
I am sensitive after all.
My words never seem to soften.
I am going home again.
Alone again.
I wish you'd stop doing this.
I know, me too.
This hurts more than ever.
Because you are older than before.
You have never done this before.
It will hurt like it's never hurt before.
Sometimes I wish I was how I was before.
Before I got a Mallory-Weiss Tear.

11/5/2023

If i die suddenly ill tell you who did it.
It was possibly the wind that cuts through skin and snow that scares my love.
Or was it my remedy to blacken my mind as the man in my apartment kept me from dreaming?
Maybe the burning liquid I bathe in at 7:30am to blink my eyes awake.
There's a chance it's the hours I have stolen from father time.
No, it's quite fruitless to talk in metaphors.
As I am my own enemy.
And I'm not eating a whole lot,
And I'm drinking a whole bunch.
Maybe death will become me.
Death becomes her or whatever the fuck they said.
The string I am holding onto is only as strong as cotton candy.
I am sorry you love it so, it dissolved in my hands before I could tell you how much I love you.
No sweeter than when you met me.

As Do The Flowers

I lose sleep quite often, never am I well rested.
My rem cycles are full of nightmarish conversations and bad
    luck.
The winter is not kind to me.
The winter seems to stick around longer than I'd like her to.
I wish I could see the flowers bloom.
Frost bites my teeth that still grin ear to ear.
My cheeks are rosy even when it's warm inside.
Inherited metabolic disorder.
I cannot escape what was built into my blood and bones
    passed down from generations on my father's side.
Does this affect my sleep?
Or is it merely a concoction of my own doing?
It's what I have to do to see the flowers bloom in December.
Don't you understand?
It's what I have to do.
I sleep beneath frozen ground, as do the flowers.
I am silent when the world peaks through my window.
I hold onto the roots in my hair for dear life.
I wish to sleep so deeply the frost cannot touch me.
So I boil my guts and come home alone.

Slipping

This morning I slipped into a new skirt with new leg warmers, an old tank top with an old cardigan.
A tired combination.
I spilled ink on my eyes and Lambrusco on my cheeks.
As I made my way to a space inhabited by a slurry of different creatures I felt myself slip.
The puddle I slipped into made my hands wet, my pupils dilated and lips chap.
As I looked at my reflection in this puddle I saw myself sink
A kind and patient woman taught me to float.
Swimming however, was mine to learn alone.
Though I know I have the skills on paper, suddenly my breath was one with the wind and my lungs burst open.
A chipped tooth can't give a love bite, a ghost can't slip into skin and smile.

11/28/2023

It was something different than anticipated.
A melted down sucker and a shared mouth full of powder.
This was the cornstarch filled night I thought would go so sour.
Nights before I felt the raised fist, the wrenching terror, the rancid touch of an expired heartbeat.
I did this more for my own curiosity than pleasure, as I expected very little.
I do not think it was the ginger that soothed my throat, I've choked on more and requested a DNR.
I'll take the morphine but DNR! it will cause shock to the body, resulting in deep profound regret.
What you asked for this morning was unavailable as it was stuck onto my skin, forgotten later for a returned favor, still stuck onto skin.
Sugar rots your teeth my love.
I licked up every drop you left me.
Be it not much as you have more of a sweet tooth than I.
Maybe it would not be so satisfying without burnt sugar, for now I'll brush my teeth and turn a blind eye on my cavities.
For now, I find the simplicity of it enthralling, palatable and enough to keep my restless tongue still.

Sometime the Other Week

Am I too unnerving for you?
I get it, unpredictability is scary.
You don't know me and I have no clue if you're the kind of person I want you to be.
Here I'll do you a favor: remove my eyes from the equation and move forward with only my tongue and teeth. (I'm practiced)
I have no idea if you're imagining my blood going straight to heaven when your hand is glued to my neck.
I like the unpredictability of that, the thought brings me peace.
With the oxygen cut off from my head I don't have to think.
I'll keep you like I keep my earrings; occasionally touching my ears.
Perfectly perfect to be hidden under my hair for a handful of nights
Then lost forever to my bedsheets and piles of clothes.

12/31/2023

Ever changing tides unfaithful to the moon.
I fell out of love and felt myself slowly sink.
Effervescent dreams of who I could be turned into a puddle of who I should be.
Who I thought I was became, "I miss the old me".
I cannot predict the future, only dwell on the past.
How was I supposed to know that I should be so fun?
Even I did not know the old me.
How dare you miss my laughter.
False claims of proclivity.
The real joys of knowing the strange me.
As seasons turn and years change I grow older still trying to escape and outlive the burdens of ancestry.
I am who I thought I'd be when I was fifteen, nobody.
Maybe this is a good thing, nobody is sought after with expectation of gratuity.
Nobody is wondered or longed for.
Nobody is empty or bursting at the seams.
Nobody is me when I become a mirror of your dreams.
What you wanted me to be is what I lovingly agreed to be.
Now I have lost the meaning of self as you perceived me.
I hope for a clean slate while I walk the world with disarray and fear.
I hope there is still a place for me at the dinner table when the time draws near.
I hope to no longer be filled with fear.
I hope to be me, sweet and caring, as my mother meant to raise me to be.
Happy new year to the old me, and good luck to the me that breathes spring air.

2/14/2024

I feel guilt because I want to be strong for the girls younger than me because I remember what it feels like to be 18 with a heart full of grief.

I feel guilt for not letting my child breathe as I drown her with your favorite liquors.

I feel the guilt of letting myself weep selfish words of how he loved me in ways that he loved no one else. (his mother told me so)

I feel the guilt of not knowing how to take care of his mother like he asked.

I feel the guilt of not saying more, of being scared to say anything at all when I could still look him in the eyes. Now I can only look at the sky and fill it with promises. (just like you, a man of my word, i will keep them)

I feel guilt for not enough "I love you-s", even though I said it every time we said goodbye.

I feel guilt for people being worried about me when I wasn't there.

If this doesn't eat me alive I think love will and maybe that's just fine.

But I do know I have to stay, I have to love, and I have to grieve.

I know you were already so proud of me, when I do everything

I dreamed I will scream it into heaven to make sure you see and hear me.

Well I might have to scream it into hell, cause there ain't no fireball in heaven.

Regression

I am feeling disconnected, like I do not belong, untrusting of everyone.

I do not feel okay, I feel like doing everything I used to do to make the world just fuzzy enough to step outside my house.

Little waves whisper in my ear to destroy everything I have built, to become 22 again.

Would it be the worst thing to breathe in what makes you draw the line, I could sit peacefully in my room knowing the loneliness I feel is material and not a figment of my imagination.

I want to be alone.

What I want more is to sit at your kitchen island and listen to your stories and tell you about the boys I'm seeing and hear your comforting words because I am falling apart and I'd rather not have anyone help me back up.

I'm independent now, I deal with it myself, there is too much guilt in making my sadness someone else's grief.

My hands are held back by a 100 year old rope that wants nothing more than to grasp at the things that could make life more beautiful.

I've always loved my uppers but I'd rather feel my body six feet under.

My chest is being stabbed over and over and over again and you would be able to stop my bleeding but the doctors couldn't stop yours.

So now here I am, sobbing on the bed I've had since I was 16, thinking about you and the poison left for me to drink.
I mixed my Budweiser with hydroxyzine and threw up in my kitchen sink.

4/30

Wide eyed, unexpected heart palpitations, trouble breathing.
Reading her body language.
You avoided touch until my eyes wandered to something more than our world.
I am guilty of sly glances, guilty of sloppy body language.
Neither of us know the new comfort in our lives, but she doesn't really seem like your type.
Silly, I feel quite silly because I am quite occupied with fitting a rose petal through a tooth gap.
Still, I cannot but feel a twinge of regret, words I let fall silent on account of being a dangerous mess.
We never really discussed things and maybe that's why I still feel like an entitled brat, unsettled scores and whatnot.
I do miss the feeling of psychotic obsession, alas it's for the best you are with a pretty girl and I lay here thinking about my mess in his bed.

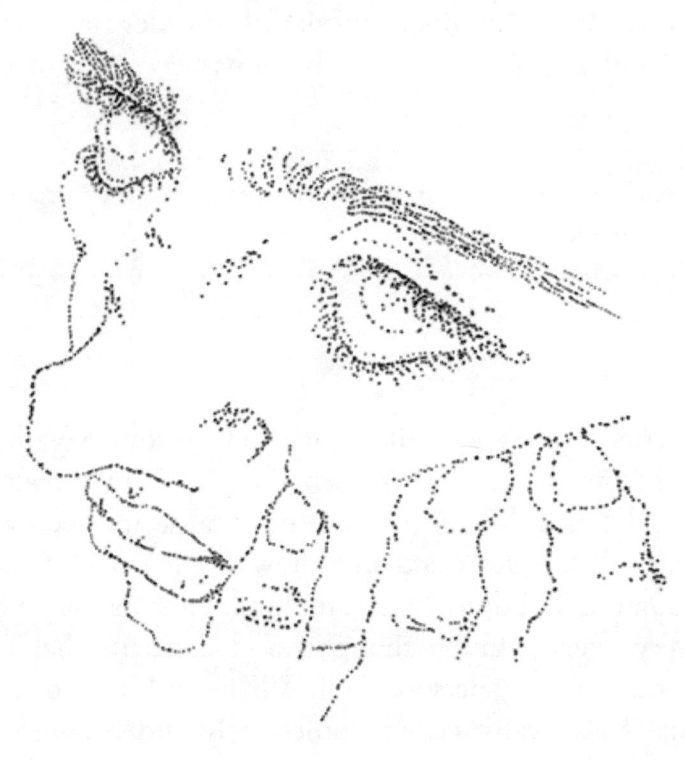

Delayed Rigor Mortis

I'm worried that I only find emotions when I'm off my meds and in industry secrets. I'm worried that the meds I take made me this way. But when I think about it, this might just be how people feel everyday. I think this is maybe how I'm supposed to feel. But who is anyone to tell me how I'm supposed to feel? The woman I pay, I suppose. I'm not numb. I still cry quite easily, but I don't FEEL anything. I think this disorder I have is much more complex and much worse than I had ever imagined.

.. - ' ...   .-.. .. -.- . --..--   ....--. . .-.   .-.. ... -.-. -.- . -..   ...
.-. --..--   -... ... -   ... --- -- . - .. -- . ...--- ... ... -   -..
--- -. ' -   .... -.-. -.- .. -. ---   -.-. .- .-. . , ..   -.. --- -. ' -   ....
. . .-..   . -- .-. .- - .... .---   .-- ..... . -.   ..   .-.. . . .-..   .-.. ..
-.- .   -. --- - .... .. -. --- ...   .-- .-. --- -. --- , ..   .-.. . . .-..   .-..
.. -.- .   .-   .-. ... .-.. ---- --- .-. .- - .... .

I'm worried I can't love like a normal person. My therapist reminded me that I haven't been IN LOVE in a really long time. And I'm a different person now cause it's been a really long time. But I don't actually know if I loved him, because again, sometimes I don't FEEL anything. I just have a lot of very loud very overwhelming thoughts and concepts that I think seem nice or like my personal hell. Whenever I start to consume someone I get really scared immediately and become mildly delusional, obsessive, and so emotionally guarded, I could be the fucking pentagon. It's like I let my weird sick and twisted brain run free while I stuff a rag in my heart's mouth.

But then I met this guy, well, I've known this guy for a while. And I might have been too honest, and I let my guard down, because I really wanted to be so in love with him.

And now I kind of feel like an asshole crawling back to this other guy who might read this (sorry). But I can't help that I like the way he taps my thighs, taught me how to yo-yo, and only sees me at night.

Rapid Succession

I got sick like his sister when her lover left.
I got angry like my mom when my dad hit her head.
I got ahold of my love and turned it into ash.
My temperature is normal, my heart rate is worthy of a phone call.
I have loved once, wanted many times, and cried more than a newborn babe.
Let me use you longer lover.
Let me feel valuable a little longer, lover.
Let me crave teeth and tongue for just a few days more.
I didn't want this so soon, in fact I liked playing on the swings.
I have no fever, just sickness of the blood like my father.
More deadly than my mother.
More alone than the chickadee when its wings faltered.

RÉPÉTER

Shoes off, "You're spiraling, do you see how you're spiraling?"
"Yes", I responded. "I have been. It's gotten bad." I cried.
"I need to change, I'm fucking up so bad."
I sob.
"I'm sorry."
"I'm going to do better."
Now I'm watching barely strangers tell each other, "I love you so much."
Circumstantial love.
I love to let things get just fuzzy enough to do it all again next week.

The problem with that is

I don't want to step in your footprints, in the places we shared full of nothing but paper and shaking foundation.
It was painful, to want you to walk through that door and lie to me.
I realized 5 hours before my birthday you never really did want me.
I can dance, I can waste time, I can love you just the way you liked it.
I could've sworn you really did like me.
No where along the way did it cross my mind I maybe loved you just a bit. Supposedly I liked you quite a lot.
Whispers left my lips talking of, "I think maybe he wants me."
No, silly little rabbit, he never cared about you. He never cared about you.
He never liked you at all, he liked what you had to offer.
The spit in my mouth, doe eyes to longingly look up, adoration of the cheapest kind.

I realized I love you

You were a tongue to eat.
A lung to hold.
Eyes to fixate.
Hands to love.
You were my renaissance and dance partner.
A fight between fists that never met.
I watched you mourn.
I watched you love.
I watched you lose.
You saw me at my worst and wanted to see me again.
Take me back to the basement where you wanted me.

This was a bad year

Every day passing seems more distant than the last.
It couldn't possibly be real.
It couldn't possibly be true.
You were stronger than most.
You were everything I am.
As you felt no fear I spoke freely, feeling untouchable,
    unforgettable and every bit capable as you.
I had the world in my hands.
My tripe trait of forgetful fever leaves me sick every day.
I am filled to the brim with hatred.
Every gift is disappointing.
Every text I would rather not read.
I have loved my birthday every year, I celebrate the whole
    month and proudly proclaim I've conquered another solar
    return. This year, six months later, i'd rather raise a glass
    alone to your heartbeat.
I wish I could've felt your wounds to better understand why
    you dug your own grave to rest.

Am I awake now?

I think I was born to fail because who is given this much joy is incapable of feeling it.

Tonight I feel like SCREAMING.

I have nothing but pure agony and a means to an end ripping apart my rib cage to shoot out of my chest.

I've given myself a headache, here's how I did it: I did not scream. I did not yank out my hair, merely tugged until I let out the saddest yelp.

I want to become too violent to be a mother so my silence is not passed onto Valentine and Lucca.

Live life with many regrets or die trying

I sit here and listen, my mouth throbbing in pain, the taste of minerals and lemon cloud my tastebuds. Everything I could ever want to say is so far from me. Even if I were to drive again I'd have to cross a bridge that hasn't been fixed in three years. These things are my fault, utterly my own doing. If I hadn't thought so much, wrote so much about my rival love, fixed on things greater than I could imagine, my reality would be much softer. I could never bring myself cradle the small bird that was dying between my finger tips. A bluejay was flying across my fields and I thought I could catch that bluejay and have her forever. I let this small bird die. I watched as its heart slowed and breath became shallow.

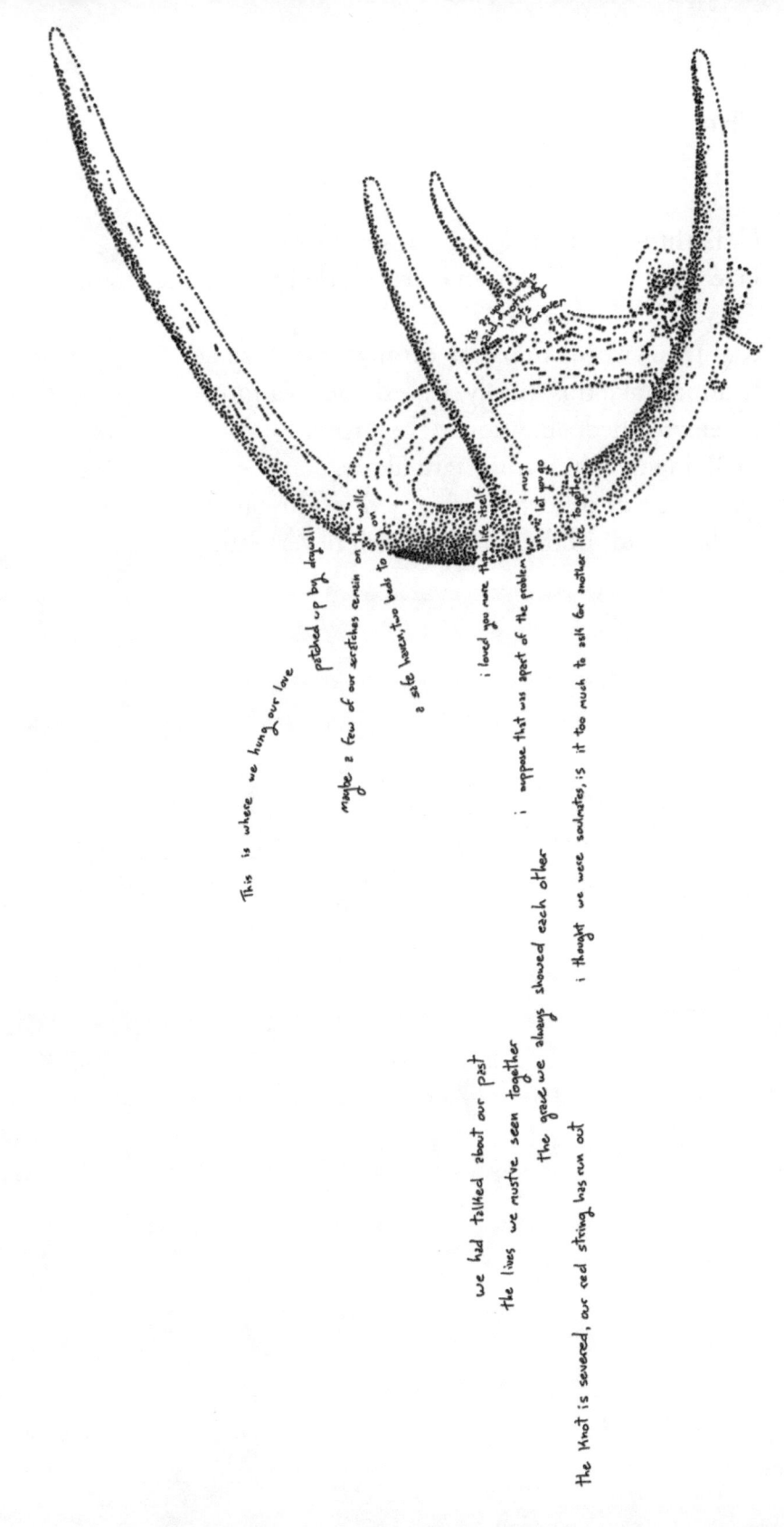

The unspeakable

Unfaithful thoughts lapped at my toes.
Five years they have been creeping up my legs like vines.
They have come to fruition.
Righteous words to pierce through my mistakes.
I cannot take this kindly, I tried and I cannot.
I feel wretched, abandoned, betrayed.
I will blame you in this light alone.
For the seeds of torture I planted in our garden, in our
    backyard, in the home we will never return to.

Final thoughts

Tonight the thoughts of forever claimed me.

Took my guts out and shamed me.

I am only the taste stuck in the back of your throat.

I am the river that escaped.

When I was young

When I was born I had a fig tree in my backyard.
My mother told me I loved blueberries but I really love figs.
She told me I'd try to reach them but my little limbs could never reach.
My mother told me I was a good baby, I never wept, screamed or thrashed.
One day she asked me what went wrong, you're only six and you're nothing like you used to be.
Now I'm 24 and I'm everything I was when I couldn't really speak for the demons that grew inside of me.
Now I'm 24 and I cannot feel anything or all I do is cry.
I pay good money to find balance, the quiet mind she liked to call it.
Every time I walk so far, miles of long conversations to myself, I put myself back in a bottle.
Every scream becomes gasping and clawing for air.
I cannot utter a peep, screams only burn my throat.
I do, however, know what went wrong, what is going wrong, why it's going wrong.
I've always had a knack for patterns and sequences.
Fall in love, psychotic love, too much, die.
Rinse, cycle, repeat, worse than the last time because now I'm 24.
I still don't know how to use a fork and knife to eat.

About Charlotte Agustin

I am a victim of an art school that taught me nothing of what I know now, but gave me the foundation to create endlessly. I was born by the race tracks in New Orleans, I lived there for barely 4 years, but I consider myself quite southern in mannerism and honesty. Writing has been a result of trying to understand myself and my flaws over the past three years. It started as something quite manic, it still is and most probably always will be.

You can discover more about Charlotte and their writing at
saintagustin.substack.com

More from Flat Sole Studio's Poetry Series

My Father's Gloves
David Spiering

My Father's Gloves touches on that most conflicted of family bonds, the one between fathers and sons. With a hauntingly painful voice, Spiering explores the burdensome yoke of a father's expectations and the struggles a son must face as he grows into manhood. His poems are accessible and wrought with emotions, his descriptions subtle in their complexity, and his pace slow yet deliberate.

Guard the Dead
John Davis
Whether chronicling the anguish of a bullet's journey through the brain or a crab's mating dance on the ocean floor, Guard the Dead demonstrates Davis's remarkable ability to render both the beauty and brutality of our existence in language alternately painful and exquisite.

A Coast Guard veteran, Davis brings an authentic voice to his verses on military life, trauma, and the perseverance of love amidst unimaginable hardship as he explores how the human spirit struggles to endure through the consequences of war.

To learn more about
Flat Sole Studio
and our other projects,
visit us at *flatsolestudio.com*
or scan the QR code below.

Sign up for our newsletter
to receive a free ebook!

www.ingramcontent.com/pod-product-compliance
Lightning Source LLC
LaVergne TN
LVHW041714060526
838201LV00043B/736